Just Above Water

Books by Louis Jenkins

Nice Fish: New and Selected Prose Poems (1995)

All Tangled Up With the Living (1991)

An Almost Human Gesture (1987)

Just Above Water

Prose Poems

by

Louis Jenkins

Holy Cow! Press · Duluth, Minnesota · 1997

Text ©1997 by Louis Jenkins
Cover Painting, *Knife Island*, acrylic on paper,
and author photograph, by Ann Jenkins.

ISBN 0-930100-75-1

Grateful acknowledgment is given to the editors and publishers of the following
publications in which some of these poems first appeared: *The Aurora, Deep Breath,
Eleventh Muse, Gettysburg Review, Great River Review, Poetry East, Poetry
International, The Prose Poem: An International Journal, Red Weather, Rosebud, Ruby,
Salted in the Shell, Solo, The Sun, The Takoma Voice, To Topio, Wolf Head Quarterly.*

This project is supported, in part, by a grant from the
Arrowhead Regional Arts Council through an appropriation from
the Minnesota State Legislature, and by generous individuals.

Holy Cow! Press books are distributed to the trade by Consortium Book Sales and
Distribution, 1045 Westgate Drive, Saint Paul, Minnesota, 55114. Our books are
also available through all major library distributors and jobbers, and through most
small press distributors, including Bookpeople and Small Press Distribution.
For personal orders, catalogs or other information, write to:

Holy Cow! Press
Post Office Box 3170
Mount Royal Station
Duluth, Minnesota 55803

Table of Contents

One

The Fishing Lure	13
Ships	14
Small Fish	15
The Ineffable	16
Spring Breakup	17
A Patch of Old Snow	18
The Ant Hill	19
Boredom	20
Motel	21
June	22
Laundromat	23
A Walk in the Woods	24
Spring Wind	25
Saints	26

Two

Three A.M.	29
Stone Arch, Natural Rock Formation	30
Beautiful Child	31
Belief	32
The Speaker	33
Yellow Hat	34
Crows at Dusk	35
Time	36
The Canoe	37
After the Storm	38
Sewing Machine	39
August Evening	40

Upon the Waters 41

Drinking Poem 42

Three

September 45

Personal History 46

The Waves 47

Gravity 48

Autumn 49

Some Notes On Writing 50

The Life of the Poet 51

The Book 52

The Couple 53

The Skiff 54

Bones 55

The Hermit of Fox Farm Road 56

November Again 57

December 58

Four

Too Much Snow 61

Jack B. Nimble 62

The Working Life 63

A Place for Everything 64

Ice 65

Paradise 66

January 67

Indecision 68

The Way Things Used to Be 69

February 70

Road Salt 71

Snow People 72

March 73

For Ann and Lars

Lake Superior

What I like best
are those rocks that
for no apparent reason
stand waist-deep
in the water and refuse
to come into shore

One

The Fishing Lure

I've spent a great deal of my life fretting over things that most people wouldn't waste their time on. Trying to explain something I haven't a clue about. It's given me that worried look, that wide-eyed, staring look. The look that wild animals sometimes have, deer for instance, trying to make sense of the situation: "What is that?" Motionless, transfixed. The same look that's on the face of the fishing lure. Stupidity? Terror? What is the right bait for these conditions? High cirrus clouds, cold front moving in. It's all a trick anyway. What is this thing supposed to be? A minnow? A bug? Gaudy paint and hooks all over. It's like bleached blond hair and bright red lipstick. Nobody *really* believes it. There isn't a way in the world I'd bite on that thing. But I might swim in just a little closer.

Ships

Now that the children are grown and their divorces are final some of my friends have moved into smaller shells somewhere up the shore. As for me, I still enjoy being all at sea, an intimate of the luminous life of the deep, bobbing up and down among ships that pass in the night, keeping my head just above water. But I don't worry, I know I'll get back to sleep when the morning fog comes in, when the Pacific fleet arrives, ghost ships from the Coral Sea. They come in silently and never cough or shuffle their feet but I know they're in the room, great hulking shapes, old and unpleasant relatives, the color of the sea, the color of the sky, gathered around my bed.

Small Fish

He's too small to keep so I remove the hook and put him back in the water. He hesitates a moment near the surface, as if not quite realizing where he is, then with a swift movement of the tail he's gone. He's back in it now, his own deep blue-green, the daily hunger and panic. He has no way of thinking about this experience. He was, then he was not, and now he is again. A seizure. But then, moments later, he's back on the surface a few feet from the boat, lying on his side, the gills working, one in the water, one in the useless air. He'd hit the bait hard and the hook had gone in deep — youthful folly, you could say, or extreme hunger, or plain bad luck. I reach out and try to grab him, but he's still too quick even in this condition. He swims down again. He's determined but the water will not have him any more. In a few seconds he's back, farther from the boat, in the domain of sunlight and hungry seagulls.

The Ineffable

Most of my life I was not paying attention, I think. That's why I remember so little — the names of lovers and intimate friends, forgotten ... the houses I lived in, the kinds of cars I drove. ... What was I thinking about, then? The ineffable, of course — I was trying to capture the ineffable. The way a person might set a live trap and catch a skunk. What now? It's a difficult situation. Certainly not the stay against confusion Frost talked about. I've heard a lot of skunk stories, and it seems to me that they all have unfortunate and ridiculous endings: baths in tomato juice and buried clothing. One story involved dynamite in the crawl space beneath a house. I believe that the person in the story was a great-uncle of mine.

Spring Breakup

Out on the big lake it's all glitter and surface, rumor and innuendo, voices that run like a shiver, out and out. . . . At the shore great slabs of ice pile up; ruined glass houses, the speculative mansions of heaven that just didn't sell and fell prey to vandals. Wherever two worlds come together damage is done. Yet the world of dreams is not much different than our own. In both one accepts cruelty and nonsense gratefully and believes. Even if you place your feet carefully and expect the worst, awakening is as sudden and unreckoned as the water.

A Patch of Old Snow

Here's a patch of snow nestled in the roots of a spruce tree. A spot the sun never touches. Mid-May and there's still snow in the woods. It's startling to come upon this old snow on such a warm day. The record of another time. It's like coming across a forgotten photograph of yourself. The stylish clothes of the period look silly now. And your haircut! Awful. You were young, wasteful, selfish, completely mistaken and, probably, no less aware than today.

The Ant Hill

On a hill overlooking the city an ant colony has come to life again now that the snow has melted. I watch the ants and make the obvious comparisons. There are workers and soldiers. There are crews clearing debris from entrances and passageways. There are ants who struggle with grass blades and sticks, objects that are much too large for them. There are others who do nothing at all except run around frantically waving their antennae. Administrators. But comparisons only go so far. No joy, no grief, no regret. . . . Apart from team spirit, it seems, the only emotional content is what we bring. If we had anything more substantial to offer, workers would surround it, as they have the corpse of this spider, and drag it down into the dark nursery.

Boredom

Nowadays I am seldom bored. There simply isn't time. Not because I am so busy, it's just that time passes more quickly as one gets older. Boredom that once lasted hours is now compacted, concentrated, so that one can experience hours of boredom in a few seconds. Intense boredom that causes one to nod off. . . . But only for five minutes. Or has it been an hour? Well, time is relative. Like that distant relative who used to be me, plodding home after school in a daydream, in a fog, so that each time he wakes he finds himself standing on the same red ant hill or running, side aching, breathless, for miles in the wrong direction with the murderous Willard brothers right behind.

Motel

The motel is very modern with fireproof doors and a sprinkler system and smoke alarms in every room. Each room has cable television with HBO. When you turn on the light in the bathroom a noisy exhaust fan comes on also. Screwed to the wall above the bed is a framed print of an old barn. Out in the hallway a faint odor of chlorine drifts up from the pool area. One of the steel doors slams shut and some children run shouting down the hall causing the entire prefabricated concrete third floor to shake. The couple in 312 are trying to get some sleep but there is a party going on in room 310. The loud talk goes on past midnight, who did what with whom and what she said and something about the real estate business (it seems they are all in the real estate business) then laughter. The motel is the last thing at the edge of town. If you slide open the opaque bathroom window you can see beyond the parking lot to an unused pasture where some papers have caught in the fence.

June

It has been raining for three days, a slow unrelenting rain; east wind, 43 degrees. An average day. The goose stands in the yard with his head under his wing. Fishing is impossible and we have no money to go shopping. The only thing left is the life of the mind. We're desperate. Rain drums on the bottom of the canoe but the message eludes us, slips away with the water that runs into ditches and creeks, over rotted wood and rusted metal, down to the big lake, where the view is water, water and watery sky, and our toes touch only water.

Laundromat

Here you are again at the laundromat late Sunday evening. There are others here: the college student with his book, the woman in tight jeans, the mother with her noisy baby. It's not like the women gathered at the river, laughing and singing. This isn't a social occasion. Everyone seems bored, exhausted, anxious to finish the wash and go home. You're here now because of poor planning. This could have been done at a more congenial time. Well, how far ahead should one plan? Next week, next year, the next ice age. . . ? Hard to believe but this is your real life, right now, watching the laundry go around. Something like watching television. And you are the star of the show, of course. Or maybe you aren't. Maybe you are only here as atmosphere, something peripheral, lending to a vague feeling of disappointment.

A Walk in the Woods

Out here in the woods I can say anything I like without fear of contradiction. I am not faced with solving any of the great problems. I have only to cross a twenty-acre patch of mixed hardwoods and spruce from one road to another without getting lost. Really, I am as free as the birds that flit from tree to tree, like the white-throated sparrow, singing "old Sam Peabody, Peabody, Peabody," or the trees that are doing their usual dance — arms extended, fingertips raised, feet firmly planted, swaying from side to side. Just across the clearing there's a group of slender aspen, all in their spring party dresses, chattering away. Now the music begins again. "Moon River." Ladies choice. That tall homely one bends over to whisper to her friend and . . . oh, hell, they're all looking straight at me.

Spring Wind

The spring wind comes through and knocks over trash cans and trees. It has something to do with warm fronts and cold fronts, I think, or with high and low pressure systems, things that I don't understand and that aren't really an explanation anyway. Ultimately the spring wind is the result of some relationship between the earth and the sun that may not be all that healthy, after all. The wind comes in a big huff, slams doors, pushes things around and kicks up the dirt. The big bully spring wind comes through on its way nowhere and, ha ha! We love it.

Saints

As soon as the snow melts the grass begins to grow. Even though the daytime high is barely above freezing, even though May is very like November, marsh marigolds bloom in the swamp and the popple trees produce a faint green that hangs under the low clouds like a haze over the valley. This is the way the saints live, no complaints, no suspicion, no surprise. If it rains, carry an umbrella, if it's cold, wear a jacket.

Two

Three A.M.

The god of three a.m. is the god of the dripping faucet, sirens, and barking dogs. He's been given titular charge of circumstances that cannot be controlled. "It's out of my hands," he says, repeatedly. He is a minor functionary, a troll that lives under a bridge. On the far side are the pastures of night where bright stars graze in the dark matter of the cosmos. He is fond of philosophic thought. "Of course, our understanding is limited. All we can do is adhere to those laws and principles that have been proven, time and again, to work." It seems there is some discrepancy in my papers. "A minor delay," he assures me. Now it's almost four.

Stone Arch, Natural Rock Formation

It is higher, more narrow, more treacherous than we imagined. And here we are in a spot where there's no going back. It has become too dangerous to continue as we have. We simply are not as sure-footed and daring as we were when we started out. There's nothing to do but sit down, carefully, straddling the rock. Once seated I'm going to turn slightly and hand the bag of groceries back to you. Then I'm going to scoot ahead a few inches and turn again. If you then lean forward carefully and hand me the bag you will be able to move ahead to the spot I previously occupied. It is a miserably slow process and we still have the problem of the steep descent on the other side. But if we are patient, my love, I believe we will arrive safely on the ground again a few yards from where we began.

Beautiful Child

People exclaim "What a pretty little girl!" But whenever a stranger speaks to her, she buries her face in her mother's lap or puts on a frown, looks away and refuses to answer. When she is alone, she sings a little song. She pushes back her long blond hair. She pretends to be a ballerina or perhaps the lady on the tight rope high above an audience that is invisible there in the dark. As she takes her first delicate step into the spotlight the crowd breaks into applause. . . . Years later her boyfriend asks "What's wrong tonight?" They have walked far down the beach and it occurs to him that she is angry. "Did I do something?" It's a question he asks frequently. "It's nothing," she says. Then there is a long silent moment. "You wouldn't understand." She looks far away across the water.

Belief

We all have certain things we believe in. Usually they don't amount to much. Some people believe that if you put a spoon in the open bottle champagne will keep its fizz. Others believe that hot water will freeze faster than cold or that when you flush a toilet in the southern hemisphere the water always turns clockwise. In the absence of anything better these beliefs serve to separate your life from others lurking in the forest around you, like scent marking. People have certain words they use, also. Words such as "paradigm," "trope," "facilitator," "objecthood". . . . Words that don't mean anything. We drop them like breadcrumbs to mark the way home — where we all intend to return one day.

The Speaker

The speaker points out that we don't really have much of a grasp of things, not only the big things, the important questions, but the small everyday things. "How many steps up to your front door? What kind of tree grows in your backyard? What is the name of your district representative? What is your wife's shoe size? Can you tell me the color of your sweetheart's eyes? Do you remember where you parked the car?" The evidence is overwhelming. Most of us never truly experience life. "We drift through life in a daydream, missing the true *richness* and *joy* that life has to offer." When the speaker has finished we gather around to sing a few inspirational songs. You and I stand at the back of the group and hum along since we have forgotten most of the words.

Yellow Hat

Nobody knows what will happen, what catastrophes, what miraculous transformations. In order to maintain faith, to plan for the future, the world must be simplified. Here is the window out of which you can see a tree, a bright red flower, green grass extending over the hill. On top of the hill, yes, there I am . . . two legs, two arms, ten fingers like sausages and a smile on my big round face. And just six inches above my yellow hat the blue sky begins.

Crows at Dusk

Just before dusk a crow lands near the top of the tall white pine on a bare branch, adjusts himself, turning one way then another, and is still. In a few moments he is joined by another crow. They greet each other with a kind of low croaking noise and touching of beaks. Then they are silent, hunkered down, feathers ruffled slightly, side by side on the branch. It seems quieter now, though the traffic on 8th Street continues unabated. The neighborhood has taken on the idea of silence. Silence, night coming on, sleep. Suddenly, without any indication of his intention, the first crow rouses himself and flies away. The second sits alone for a moment or two then flies also, in a different direction.

Time

All of a sudden, for no apparent reason, my wrist watch, which is lying on the bedside table, begins to tick louder. As if it wanted my attention. What is it? What could a watch possibly want? Cleaning? A new battery? Or is it Time calling attention to itself. *Tempus fugit*, and all that. No, it wants . . . *something*. Time is a big semi-domestic animal, confused from too long with humans, like a big dog that whines to be let out then immediately barks to be let back in. He doesn't know what he wants anymore than we do. Want to go for walk big boy? Yeah, yeah! He pulls on the leash, first one way then another. It's a constant tug-of-war. He wants to be turned loose, to run around in circles sniffing at everything. He doesn't care if you come too. If you can keep up.

The Canoe

Of the things I own I like my canoe best, I think. So light-weight and easy to portage. Delicate, it seems, fragile as memory, but really it's quite strong. Eighteen feet long, it will carry two, sometimes three, adults and their gear, and it's amazing the amount of baggage people bring. Even fully loaded with only a few inches of freeboard, the canoe moves gracefully over the water. Remarkably stable given the circumstance. It can handle most whitewater but I don't need whitewater. The river at its best, single-minded and self-righteous, is enough. I like it when the river flows straight and silvery for half-a-mile or more before it bends and disappears in the trees.

After the Storm

The stream is in turmoil today, running bank-full with brown, muddy water, making a terrible roar, an echo of last night's thunderstorm. Despite the water's headlong rush there's a lot of uncertainty here. The surrounding forest is silent, depressed, saturated and dripping beneath an overcast sky. A piece of a tree limb, probably broken off in the storm, has fallen into the river and is stalled in one of the pools above the falls. It bumps around in the foam-covered eddies and back-currents, slowly circling, snagging occasionally on the rocks, looking awkward and confused, like an adolescent confronted finally with the adult world. The stick is bullied and pushed by the water. Then chance sends the branch out into the main current and it bolts downstream like a frightened animal. As if a split-second decision had been made. As if there were a choice in this matter.

The Sewing Machine

When she sat down in the morning to sew she discovered that her machine was completely out of adjustment. Obviously someone had gotten in during the night and fooled around with it. One afternoon she sat down on the couch for only a minute or two. Then something caused her to wake with a start. There was a man sitting right next her! Her waking caused him to wake also. When he saw her he got up and out of there in a hurry! Locks were no good though she had them changed twice. She began blocking the doors by wedging a chair under the doorknob of each. That was a problem whenever she passed out — once she lay there on the kitchen floor for an hour before the police were able to break in. The police. A lot of good they were. Criminals loose all over town. What could an old woman do alone, trapped inside her house?

August Evening

A cloud of tiny insects hovers just above the edge of the point where the land drops away steeply to the Lake. There must be a thousand of them flying every which way in a sexual frenzy. Yet the cloud keeps its integrity. It's the world's largest singles bar! There's some selection process at work here. It's obvious that not just anyone will do. But it works. Mated pairs, tail to tail, drop out of the cloud, sinking together to the ground. The weight of it brings them down while the others continue the dance, round and round in the warm evening air.

Upon the Waters

After a week of gray skies a single shaft of sunlight breaks through the clouds over the lake and illuminates a small area of surface water with the holy faith, inaccessible to those of us on shore. When the *Manistee* began to break up, the sailors took the only door that opened and went down.

Thirty fathoms down fish patrol the slimy wreckage, and rise quickly into the light, into the commingling of water and air. As quickly as that, in that moment your attention focused somewhere out there, the baby drifted away. His diaper changed, his bottle filled, he rides the waves in his basket like a king, slightly annoyed and a bit uncomfortable.

Drinking Poem

Because I have no one else
to drink with tonight
I go down to the lakeshore
and take the water
and the moon for my companions.
Already the moon is high
and the water, stirred by the wind,
becomes loquacious.
It's the same old story.
The water sculpts these rocks.
It takes a thousand years,
smoothing and polishing.
There's no money in it,
so far from the major markets.
As I listen I grow drowsy.
Water on the rocks . . .
What's to be done?
What's to be done?

Three

September

for Phil Dentinger

One evening the breeze blowing in the window turns cold and you pull the blankets around you. The leaves of the maples along Wallace Avenue have already turned and whoever it was you loved does not come around anymore. It's all right. Things change with the cycle of the seasons and evolve. A mistake, a wrong turn takes one elsewhere. But perhaps there are forces other than chance at work here. Perhaps a person changes merely out of boredom with the present condition. Perhaps our children, from a desire to become simply other than what we are, grow feathers, learn to breathe underwater or to see in the dark.

Personal History

One has a feeling of having not lived life to its fullest, having not really accomplished anything and at the same time there is a feeling of regret for past sins, those things one would like to undo. And all the while the years passing, passing . . . turning to decades, centuries. Think of the Hittites, at one point the hottest power in the world, a practical, down-to-earth people but one that did little, finally, to advance human civilization. What would a Hittite say if you met on the street?

"Listen, I'd like to apologize for those unwanted advances I made."

"That's all right. It was a long time ago."

"Nevertheless, I feel uneasy about it. It was rude and selfish of me. It's just that you were so. . . ."

"It's OK, really. I can honestly say I never think of it."

The Waves

The east wind has risen today and the waves rise up. Praise to all rising up! To the life that seemed might never return after so many days of dead calm. The wind sends wave after wave scudding toward the shore where the ragged grass clings to the rock. Waves. I recognize some of them. They lift from the void, white-haired but determined, as if each had a purpose, a private destiny, someplace to go (brunch? a board meeting?). Once the savior walked across the water to give each wave, personally, a hand up. Perhaps he is returning even now, but the road to the shore is long, long. . . . The waves break and fall face forward, losing touch, losing credibility, losing all pretense of dignity.

Gravity

It turns out that the drain pipe from the sink is attached to
nothing and water just runs right onto the ground in the
crawl space underneath the house and then trickles out
into the stream that passes through the backyard. It turns
out that the house is not really attached to the ground but
sits atop a few loose concrete blocks all held in place by
gravity, which, as I understand it, means "seriousness." Well,
this is serious enough. If you look into it further you will
discover that the water is not attached to anything either
and that perhaps the rocks and the trees are not all that
firmly in place. The world is a stage. But don't try to move
anything. You might hurt yourself, besides that's a job for
the stagehands and union rules are strict. You are merely a
player about to deliver a soliloquy on the septic system to a
couple dozen popple trees and a patch of pale blue sky.

Autumn

Black crows wheeling overhead . . . the shocking blue sky above the gold leaf autumn trees.

It's one of those roads that starts off purposefully but most likely trails off into a jumble of popple and alder. Remember this is hunting season, bullets flying everywhere. Best to sing or shout as you go along.

This world we love and cannot hold, this world we love and mistreat, that mistreats us, that crumbles at a touch, that drifts away like smoke. . . .

There are sounds out of our range, too high, too low. There is light beyond the visible spectrum. Our brains are unable to make sense of our own lives. And my hair goes every which way.

It's a bad system. Who's responsible for this mess anyway? Jenkins. I recognize the plodding style.

Some Notes on Writing

Contrary to the pronouncements of certain notable poets it makes no difference whether you write with a pencil or a pen. Notebooks are another matter. You will find that in certain notebooks less than half the pages are of any use, others must be abandoned almost immediately. There's no useful formula. Notebooks are a matter of trial and error.

You sit woodenly at the table, notebook open, pencil near at hand, awaiting the arrival of the muse. Because you are staring into the middle distance you haven't noticed that the muse has already flown into the room and hangs as if suspended by monofilament, twisting slightly in the warm air currents. In order to come beneath her hand, that is outstretched in blessing, it may be necessary to move your table to another part of the room.

Brother bear has caught cold and gone to sleep in his den. Brother fox is rummaging in the fallen leaves for airline tickets. Everybody and his brother is going about his business. No one is waiting for you to finish this but where else will you live?

The Life of the Poet

I once believed that behind all the things I did, or more often, failed to do, there was a great moral purpose, or at least some coherent principle, a *raison d'être*. If there is such a principle it has never become quite clear to me. Instead, over the years, I have managed to take a random selection of bad habits and herd them together into a life. Also, in order to disguise my absolute laziness I have mastered the age-old art of appearing to be productive when, actually, *this* is the only thing I'm doing. (Republicans suspected as much all along.) Someone comes up to my desk and I get busy scribbling, totally preoccupied. "What? Oh, I'm sorry. . . ." In my haste to appear industrious I find I have written ". . . and herd them together into a *wife*."

The Book

Every night I read the same paragraph, the words of fire, the perfect symmetry! But it is impossible to hold. My eyes close and the book falls from my hands. . . . Sometime later in the night I wake, long enough to switch off the lamp and pull the blankets around me. By morning I've forgotten everything. Outside a gray workday drizzle is falling and the text is flat, uninspired. At night on the page between awake and asleep, the world makes perfect sense. There we meet again for the first time and you take my hand.

The Couple

They no longer sleep quite as well as they did when they were younger. He lies awake thinking of something that happened a long time ago, turning uncomfortably from time to time, pulling on the blankets. She worries about money. First one and then the other is awake during the night, in shifts, as if keeping watch, though they can't see very much in the dark and it's quiet. They are sentries at some outpost, an abandoned fort somewhere in the middle of the great plains where only the wind is a regular visitor. Each stands guard in the wilderness of an imagined life in which the other sleeps untroubled.

The Skiff

Jim was at the tiller holding her into the wind, moving us along while I lifted the net. Then we began to drift. The net was damn near to pull my arms off and I thought damnit Jim, pay attention to what the hell you're doing. I turned my head to yell at him and he wasn't there! I dropped the net, scrambled back past the engine compartment and grabbed the tiller, all the while looking around like crazy to see if I could spot Jim's head above the waves . . . but there was nothing, not even a gull, just a few clouds far away on the eastern horizon. I circled back along the net yelling my head off. I cut the engine to listen. The quiet was strange after the engine noise, the sound of the waves lapping against the hull. Not much of a wind, two foot waves, just a breeze out of the southwest. It seemed impossible. I must have spent hours going around in circles, calling out, even after I knew it was useless. There was nothing, no sign. Nothing but water and sky. It must have been the water took him, but for all I know it was the sky. Then I noticed the half peanut butter sandwich on the seat beside me. It startled me as if it had been a snake. There was a bite out of one end. Jim's jacket was gone. That sandwich was the only thing to prove Jim had ever been here at all.

Bones

The leaves have fallen, the geese have flown south and your hair has turned gray. Most of the people who knew you when you were a baby are dead now. Whatever it was caused them to stand up and walk around as if they knew where they were going has flown also. Something caused them to hesitate, turn back to the house, then begin again, slamming the screen door behind. That impulse has gone. Nothing remains now but bones, the skeptical bones. Soon snow will come to cover them again. No one has coffee ready, there are no fields to plow and they know all about you, shuffling around in the dry leaves. "It's only that kid up there, no reason to get up."

The Hermit of Fox Farm Road

Perhaps one's existence is dependent on the recognition of that existence by others. One ceases to be because one is no longer perceived. Like the tree that falls in the forest that makes a noise only if there are ears to hear. If the human attention span were longer people would live longer lives. The way we are, we can hold a concept for only for a brief period. Then our minds wander, we become bored. We want something new on the Top Forty. Yet it seems to me that I'm still here — so perhaps she remembers, (no one else would) though we spoke only those few times and nothing I tried to say came out right. Only dimly now she imagines what I am, a stick figure, nearly invisible among the sticks of these woods.

November Again

November again and the snow comes sudden and heavy. This is what we like best. This is what we paid our money for. Snow on snow, all day and all night, everything muffled, distant. Tomorrow, no school, no work, no worship service, no visitation of the sick, the poor, the widows or the orphans. Whatever it was, nothing can be done about it now. Your old position has been filled. Your footsteps have been filled. The roads are filled, drifted shut. All directions are obliterated in the heavy snowfall.

December

These winter days are so short, pale, a lingering twilight between the long nights; a scrap of paper shoved under the door into a dark apartment. A note, a thinly veiled threat perhaps: "Only ten shopping days 'til Christmas." No, something else. What can be said in such a small space? Outside, the streetlights are coming on. "I was able to get here at last. Sorry to have missed you."

Four

Too Much Snow

Unlike the Eskimos we only have one word for snow but we have a lot of modifiers for that word. There is too much snow, which, unlike rain, does not immediately run off. It falls and stays for months. Someone wished for this snow. Someone got a deal, five cents on the dollar, and spent the entire family fortune. It's the simple solution, it covers everything. We are never satisfied with the arrangement of the snow so we spend hours moving the snow from one place to another. Too much snow. I box it up and send it to family and friends. I send a big box to my cousin in California. I send a small box to my mother. She writes "Don't send so much. I'm all alone now. I'll never be able to use so much." To you I send a single snowflake, beautiful, complex and delicate; different from all the others.

Jack B. Nimble

The only light is the light you carry. You can feel the darkness coming up close behind. If you turn suddenly the darkness jumps back, the way the lion retreats momentarily from the desperate wildebeest. Once you were a beacon. Once you set the candlestick atop your head and did the rumba, the cha cha, the limbo, until the wee hours of the morning. You hold that candle so carefully in front of you that it makes strange shadows and lines across your face but, honestly, I've never seen you looking better. And that new suit, I think, works wonders.

The Working Life

Unless you have a boss who is really a jerk, the job is a minor discomfort, like shoes that are just a bit too tight. Most of us go through our work days mechanically without thinking about what we are doing. "Hello. Anybody in there?" Our minds are elsewhere. "Hello, hello" the burglar calls out. Nobody home. You've become part of the vast, undulating daydream, swaying in the wind like prairie grass. The burglar breaks the pathetic lock, empties the contents of the drawers, pulls the books from the shelves. . . . There's your whole life strewn across the floor. The burglar steals the t.v., and the stereo and in return leaves new Visa and Mastercards with your name on them. You won't know this until hours later. This time of year we go to work in darkness, return home in darkness.

A Place for Everything

It's so easy to lose track of things. A screwdriver, for instance. "Where did I put that? I had it in my hand just a minute ago." You wander vaguely from room to room, having forgotten, by now, what you were looking for, staring into the refrigerator, the bathroom mirror . . . "I really could use a shave. . . ."

Some objects seem to disappear immediately while others never want to leave. Here is a small black plastic gizmo with a serious demeanor that turns up regularly, like a politician at public functions. It seems to be an "intregal part," a kind of switch with screw holes so that it can be attached to something larger. Nobody knows what. This thing's use has been forgotten but it looks so important that no one is willing to throw it in the trash. It survives by bluff, like certain insects that escape being eaten because of their formidible appearance.

My father owned a large, three-bladed, brass propeller that he saved for years. Its worth was obvious, it was just that it lacked an immediate application since we didn't own a boat and lived hundreds of miles from any large bodies of water. The propeller survived all purges and cleanings, living, like royalty, a life of lonely privilege, mounted high on the garage wall.

Ice

Walking on the icy pavement demands your attention. You have to learn to read the color, the texture, learn where you can safely step, learn to watch for the smooth, almost invisible ice or ice hidden by a light dusting of snow — suddenly you're flat on your back. Children don't worry about it. Their bodies are flexible and resilient and they have a shorter distance to fall. They fall, jump up and continue running. It's nothing. If a person of my age and size falls it makes a considerable impact. It's painful and embarrassing. Once I fell in front of the hardware store downtown, just like that, both feet straight out in front of me. Passersby gave me a strange look, not concern, more like disbelief. "What is this guy doing?" The very old, women on high-risk shopping trips, old men shovelling snow on rooftops, seem to have forgotten the ice entirely. If their frail bodies were caught by the least wind they would skitter and clatter over the hard surface for miles.

Paradise

January finally drags into February and one fumbles with numb fingers at the ordinary knots and hooks of life. People are irritable, difficult. Some days you want to stay in bed with the covers over your head and dream of paradise. A place where the warm sea washes the white sand. There are a few palm trees on the higher ground, many brightly colored fish in the lagoon, waves breaking on the reef farther out. No one in sight. Occasionally an incredibly large, split-second shark darkens the clear water. Sea birds ride the wind currents, albatross, kittiwake, . . . and pass on. Day after day, sea wind and perfect sky. . . . You make a big heap of driftwood on the beach.

January

Daytime highs are well below zero. The air is absolutely clear and dry, the wind sharp, precise. We walk about in our bulky clothes like spacemen or old-fashioned divers on the bottom of the sea. The snow crunches underfoot. Now, above a single bare birch tree in the middle of a field of untrodden snow, the evening star appears in a most extraordinary blue sky. Everything is hard-edged, clear-cut. A perfect world. The sky is the exact color of Mary Beth Anderson's eyes. Beautiful, perfect. Perfect hair and perfect teeth. It always seemed that she knew exactly what she wanted and where she was going, that she had planned her life in detail. One thing I know for sure, she would have had no time for anyone who dressed the way we do.

Indecision

People died or moved away and did not return. Things broke and were not replaced. At one time he had owned a car and a telephone. No more. And yet somehow, things did not become more simple. Then one night, roused from sleep he stepped out naked into the below zero winter night, into the clear midnight and 20 billion stars. Nothing stirred, not a leaf, nothing out there, not the animal self, not the bird-brained self. Not a breath of wind yet somehow the door slammed shut locking behind him and knocking the kerosene lantern to the floor. Suddenly the whole place was afire. What to do? Should he try to make the mile-long run through the woods over hard-crusted snow to the nearest neighbor or just stick close to his own fire and hope that someone would see the light? The cabin was going fast. Flames leaped high above the bare trees.

The Way Things Used To Be

When we moved out here thirty years ago there weren't so many paved roads. There were fewer houses, fewer people. There weren't so many lights. Could be there's more of everything now. It seems to me we get more snow now than we used to. We were a long way from town in those days but we didn't see so many animals. There were tracks, only suggestions. . . . I'm sure we see more moose nowadays. It was quiet. There was the wind in the spruce trees that seemed sometimes as if it were saying something, but wasn't. Often on clear nights you'd see the aurora. Basically, though, there was nothing out here. That's changed. It's hard to explain the way things used to be. It's hard to find words to explain the loss of nothing.

February

for Michael Van Walleghen

Snow falls upon snow. It piles up on the roads, mile after gray mile of it catches in the wheelwells of the car. It piles up like debt, like failure, and, as your mother pointed out, you've put on a few pounds since Christmas. Now in February the winter seems permanent, glacial. Each snow-fall is more a feeling than an external event, a heaviness, shortness of breath. . . . You wake in a panic, tearing at the blankets. . . . It's only a cat. A large house cat. You've wakened in an overheated room in a strange house with the family cat sleeping on your chest. You are a guest, you don't belong here. Heart pounding, you want to be on your way. But it's the middle of the night, in winter. There's no place to go. . . . You won't be here very long. Relax. Nothing has changed. You are who you've always been, only more so.

Road Salt

A big orange truck comes along spreading sand and salt on the icy road. Sand, salt, freshly ground pepper . . . with a few minutes cooking the road is ready, done to a turn. You can be on your way. But salt is not content just to eat the snow and ice. It starts in on your automobile. Rust spots develop, then holes where the salt has eaten through. Though you wash the car scrupulously salt finds secret, hidden spots and eventually the floor falls dumping the passengers and their luggage in the road. Eventually the whole car collapses into a heap of rusty powder and scale. A white, salty residue gathers on your shoes as you walk away. You could repair those rust spots now, before the worst happens, but life is short. Who has time for that?

Snow People

Being mostly water as we are, it's not so bad living in a cold climate like this one. It gives you a certain solidity. Cold feet, the icy handshake, the cold shoulder, the frozen countenance, shouldn't be thought of as ill-will but as a kind of preservation. When life touches life more heat is given off than is ordinarily healthy. Just look at the way my ears have begun to droop from the things whispered there. There are fires without and fires within. It won't do any good to throw yourself into the fire, you can't become the flames. You will end up as a small puddle of water that someone else steps over at the end of winter.

March

It hadn't occurred to me until someone at work brought it to my attention, that this winter has been going on for eleven years. I said, "That can't be. Surely not." But then I got thinking about it. It was eleven years ago November we moved into this house. You remember, snow was just beginning and we had so much trouble getting the refrigerator down the driveway and through the door. Danny was eight and we got him a sled for Christmas. It's amazing how one gets concerned with other things and the time just goes by. Here it is March and now that I've noticed it, the snow has begun to melt a little. During the day there's water running in the street. It's like a bird singing in a tree that flies just as you become aware of it. When you think about it, the world, cold and hard as it is, begins to fall apart.

Louis Jenkins was born in Oklahoma and lived in the Southwest until 1971 when he married Ann Jacobson and moved to Duluth, Minnesota where they still live. They have a son, Lars. Louis Jenkins' poetry has appeared in a number of literary magazines and poetry anthologies. He is the author of several books including *Nice Fish*: New and Selected Prose Poems (Holy Cow! Press, 1995) which was awarded the 1995 Minnesota Book Award for Poetry.